THE GREA~~~~ ~~ ~~~ TIME: LEBRON JAMES

THE STORY OF HOW LEBRON JAMES BECAME THE MOST DOMINANT PLAYER IN THE NBA

Presented By:

LESSONS IN LEADERSHIP INSTITUTE

LessonsInLeadership.Institute

Copyright © 2018

INTRODUCTION

No single player captures the essence of domination like LeBron James. From his time as a rising High School Senior where he was featured on the cover of Sports Illustrated to the 2018 season where he almost single-handedly carried his team to the NBA Finals, LeBron James has always been at the center of the spotlight.

In this book, we will look at LeBron's journey and how he has emerged as the top player of All Time. With special focus spent on not just that what he did, but how and why he did it, this makes for an inspiring read for the casual and diehard fan as well as the aspiring basketball star.

Learn how LeBron changed his life from a boy in Akron, Ohio to the most dominant sportsman in the world.

TABLE OF CONTENTS

THE FOUNDATION OF A LEGACY

How can we mention basketball without mentioning LeBron James? James, a man who in his early years made reasonable impact won most awards in the history of basketball. In fact, fashion stars cannot claim to have at least a single piece of LeBron's shoes or clothing induced by Nike in their closet. This is how much impression LeBron has had in the whole world at large. Without mincing words, LeBron is not just a name, it is a brand. A brand which virtually everyone wants to relate to, use as a figurative head for offering prayers, parent's wish for their children's future and in short, a very big source of motivation. But did James suddenly attain fame overnight without breaking a sweat? Was he a child born with a silver spoon in his mouth, did he become famous without putting up a fight for survival? How did he become a center focus of motivation and entreaty for everyone who is trying to be inspired? All these are what we will have to discuss in subsequent chapters. So take a deep breath and enjoy this beautiful masterpiece.

Life has never been rosy. Every successful person has a story to tell regardless of what they have been or passed through and achieved. There have been days when these people felt lost and alone in the whole world without anyone interceding for them. However, that turned out to be the turning point for their career and life generally. But during those times, every idea of theirs sounded very awkward to anyone hearing it, but these people have had their own fair share of life and have subsequently written their own inspirational biographies themselves. They held on to their skills, ideas, and passions and successively executed them without having to fear what others would think about them and thereafter became successful in their different ventures. This is when their idea played out more significantly and made more sense to others, which is another reason why this book about LeBron James will inspire to know where your passion lies and what you should do to make it not just a dream but also how to actualize them.

There is nothing compared to having firsthand taste of greatness. They make it more certain that there is more than a glimpse of greatness we've seen in our fictitious moments. Stories that in point of fact materialized can be just as, or even more amazing.

The few successful people we presently see as bosses of their specialty were once simply people with fantasy — to influence music, to play basketball, or football, to compose, to make people laugh, to change the world. What's more, through their self-portrayal, we can get a look into the life and the battle that occurred before the actualizing their goals.

These stories can be found in practically every field — from biographies of sport people, entrepreneurs diaries, artists, comics, journalists, to government officials — whatever you seek to be, you will always be inclined toward somebody's comparative objective.

Success is not a destination, it is a life long journey filled with ups and downs that tests every person that goes down its path. For some, perusing a rousing book is sufficient inspiration to take a stab at accomplishing their fantasies. Others look for the direction of a guide, similar to a motivational speaker or an educator, to goad their drive for progress. .

Behind each fruitful individual are people who got it going, and this isn't really restrictive to those associated actually to somebody's life. There are incalculable people in general society eye who, through their activities, fill in as motivations. Be they on-screen characters, performers, creators, trailblazers, or business pioneers, these individuals embody accomplishment in each part of their lives—not just their accomplishments.

Before now, have you been feeling that inward drive to look for a greater course? To begin with, your action would determine all these. Try learning about an individual you can relate to and see how you can link them to their personal life, thus taking them as your mentor. Take for example, LeBron James, who was an exceptional basketball player during and stood out from the different appealing people of his opportunity.

It is frequently said that achievement happens when planning meets opportunity. Presently, opportunities will introduce themselves with time, yet how are you treating yourself through the majority of the time spent in anticipation of achieving your objectives meanwhile?

Is it right to conclude that you are giving yourself acknowledgment for the work and the vitality that it takes to wind up a more effective person?

A noteworthy part of the achievement condition needs to do with regarding yourself. Treating yourself with generosity and consolation along your life travel. It's critical to commend all triumphs expansive towards satisfying your fantasies.

Everything starts with perceiving that you are an effective individual and your victories can just go up from here.

Folks and young ladies: Just having the assurance to seek after your joy, your objectives and your fantasies is an enormous accomplishment in itself.

It takes a staggering measure of valor to get up each morning and continue moving and spurring yourself to progress in the direction of the existence that you've generally envisioned living.

The planning of some portion of the achievement condition, ought to be commended, for progress isn't just a goal. Success doesn't happen in a day. It has an inseparable tie to your individual decisions, activities and encounters. Regardless of how they seem.

Success is linked with consistency with your identity and how you react to each condition that happens in your life.

In case you're searching for a touch of motivation to enable you to encourage your specialty, or in the event that you basically require another book to peruse and are a major fanatic of LeBron James there's most likely something here for you.

LeBron James has this to say concerning success and being successful, - "Warren Buffett told me once and he said always follow your gut. When you have that gut feeling, you have to go with don't go back on it."

A CAREER OF EXCELLENCE

If you have not heard of LeBron Raymone James, then your social life is probably not in an updated terms. Regardless it wouldn't be out of place to pen down some few things about the famous basketball player. LeBron James is a professional player who has won virtually every award that a basketball player can win. Many people have considered him as the best basketball player of all time because of his sporting prowess and passionate way of playing basketball. His basketball exploit includes winning the NBA Most Valuable Player Awards four times, two Olympic gold medals, three NBA Finals MVP Awards, an NBA scoring title, three All-Star Game MVP awards, and also holds the record of the highest scoring player in the NBA playoffs. The player has twelve All-NBA first team title, five All-Defensive First Team honors and featured in fourteen All-star game appearances.

However, the boy James wasn't born a superstar but rose through the ranks with hard work and determination. James was birthed by a sixteen-year old mother, Gloria on the 30th of December, 1984 in a small town of Akron in Ohio. Reports have it that James's father, Anthony McClelland was a criminal on the streets of America and just a casual boyfriend to his mother, Gloria. James upbringing is leathered with quite a lot of struggle moving from one apartment to another in Akron while his mother tried all within her means to secure a regular job to make ends meet for her young son and herself.

You see sometimes we are allowed to go through the hurdles of life to prepare us properly for the best in the future. We cannot deny the fact that there is something called destiny but often times, we are the makers of such destiny from how well we handle our present life impediments with the choices we make. Making the right choices and setting priorities right will put us on the very edge of achieving our age-long desires, thus meaning we can always try to complete that which we want and then surrender the rest to fate and destiny. This can be said to be the case of LeBron. At the point when Gloria noticed that her son would be better off in a more comfortable environment, she allowed him to be with the Frank Marcher's family, who at that time was a local football coach and also allowed James to play for the kid's basketball team at age nine.

At a very young age, LeBron has already featured in the Amateur Athletic Union (AAU) b-ball for the Upper East Ohio Shooting Stars. The team, led by James and his teammates, Sian Cotton, Willie McGee and Dru Joyce III, however excelled both locally and on national level. The group was very close and seemed inseparable, while they promised to go to the same high school which they did as they went to St. Vincent– St. Mary High School, an overwhelmingly white private Catholic school.

Being a person driven with zeal to be a professionally, James went ahead to feature in the high school (St. Vincent– St. Mary High School) basketball team which led to his vigorously touting in the national media as a NBA future hotshot.

Time saw James join the Cleveland Cavaliers in 2003 as the first draft pick. Within a short time, he became a league star and finished up his first season by winning the NBA Rookie of the Year Award. He thereafter set himself as one of the biggest stars in the NBA with numerous honors, including being honored with the NBA Most Valuable Player Award in 2009 and 2010. Nonetheless, after failing to meet championship hopes as the expected by the media, fans, and himself, James had to leave Cleveland in 2010 as a free player to sign with the Miami Heat. This move featured as a hit news in a report by News giant, *ESPN, as* **The Decision,** which turned out to be one of America's biggest sport moves in history.

While at Miami, James won his first NBA championship in 2012, and won another in the second year. He was named league MVP and NBA Finals MVP in both championship years. In 2014, James refused to sign a new contract with Miami after four seasons and decided to re-sign with the Cavaliers. In 2016, Cavaliers Cleveland led by LeBron won their first NBA championship vanquishing the Golden State Warriors to end the team's 52-year pro athletics title dry spell. In 2018, he signed with Lakers.

HUMBLE BEGINNINGS: THE HIGH SCHOOL YEARS

During James first year in the high school basketball team, he had an averaged 21 points and 6 rebounds per game. The school team (Fighting Irish) went ahead to win the Division III state title undefeated and making a record as the first boy's high school team not to have lost a game in a season. As a sophomore player he continued to shine averaging a team high 25.2 points and 7.2 rebounds with 5.8 assists and 3.8 steals per game. Since St. Vincent-St. Mary was becoming famous nationally through their streak, they had to opt to playing at the University of Akron's 5,492-seat Rhodes Arena for home games so that they could meet up with the ticket demands from fans, scouts, alumni, the college and the likes, who were coming in to watch James display his expertise in the big game of basketball. In the league season that followed they remained undefeated, The Fighting Irish made another impressive record of winning 26–1 and became the state champions for a second consecutive time. LeBron James to everyone was just too much of a wonder kid and this made him earn the nickname Ohio, Mr. Basketball and also earned a place in the Unites States Today, All-USA first team, and thus becoming the first sophomore to achieve such feat.

During James's junior years in high school, he had already gained the attention of the US media. He appeared on the cover pages of SLAM Magazine and was alluded to as the best high school basketball player by writer Ryan Jones. This wasn't all as James was a roaring fire daring anyone to quench. He also appeared on another magazine, Sport Illustrated, and then becoming the first high school player to achieve that.

James seem to be upping his game every season as he was named Ohio Mr. Basketball once again winning an average of 29 points, 5.7 assists, 8.3 rebounds, and 3.3 steals in every game played.. This time, he was not only selected to become one of USA Today All-USA First Team, he was the first junior boy to win the boys' basketball Gatorade National Player of the Year. The third season only saw St. Vincent-St. Mary loosing 4 games from the 27 games played with a loss in the Division II championship game. James was a man of vision who hated the loss but was able to keep his focus on the road ahead.

James year in senor classes in the high school was more eventful than the junior classes. He spent a good amount of it travelling round the country playing some elite games against top ranked teams which included a game against Oak Hill Academy which was aired by ESPN2 TV. Many cable companies at that time were all looking for a way to build on LeBron's status but it seemed Time Warner Cable, made the noble move by offering St. Vincent-St. Mary's a pay-per-view subscription basis through the season.

All this while LeBron wasn't doing bad for himself as he still had an average of 31.6 points, 4.6 assists, 9.6 rebounds, and 3.4 steals in every game, thus winning him the Ohio Mr. Basketball and chosen among the USA Today All-USA First Team for a first-time record of holding the title in a third consecutive year. He also was given the Gatorade National Player of the Year for the second year in a roll.

He partook in three year-end high school ball all star games—the EA Games Roundball Classic, the Jordan Capital Classic, and the McDonald's All-American game —losing his National University Athletic Affiliation (NCAA) qualification and making it official that he would enter the 2003 NBA draft. Virtually every basketball expert, scout, and author at that time commented that LeBron James left high school as truly outstanding and most built up prospects ever.

Still in his senior years, it was impossible to mention sports and not mention LeBron. When he clocked 18 years old, his mother gifted him a Hummer H2 from a loan she got from using LeBron's future gaining power as a NBA hotshot. This incited probation from the Ohio High School Athletic Affiliation (OHSAA) in light of the fact that its rules expressed that no amateur may acknowledge any present worth over $100 as a reward for athletic execution. James was cleared of any bad behavior since he had the gift was from his mother, a close relative and not from an external source. Later, James got some shirts claimed to be worth $845 from a clothing store, thereby formally damaging OHSAA governs and bringing about him being stripped of his high school sports qualification. James claimed the decision and his punishment was in the end dropped to a two-game suspension, enabling him to play the rest of the year. The Irish were likewise compelled to relinquish one of their wins, their single loss that season. After suspension, James scored a career high 52 points in his very first game. His team went on to win the Division II championship, which served as his third division title in four years.

Other Sports

Generally, most people didn't know that LeBron James played a wide beneficiary for St. Vincent-St. Mary's football team and was enlisted by some Division I programs, including Notre Dame. During his sophomore year, he was the named first team all-state, and being a junior, he led the Fighting Irish to the state tournament. James stopped playing football when he broke his wrist amid an AAU b-ball game. However, some football pundits, high school mentors, and previous and current players still till this very day hypothesized that James would have played in the National Football League if he continued playing.

LIVING UP TO EXPECTATIONS: LIFE IN THE NBA

James started his professional career from his home town team, the Cleveland Cavaliers. In fact, he was the first choice after he scaled through the 2003 NBA draft. The first season he got there, James score 25 points even as a rookie against the Sacramento Kings, which set an NBA record of the most points scored by an uprising player. He continued in fine form till the end of the season. During this time, he was awarded the NBA Rookie of the Year. With an average of 20.9 points, 5.9 assists in every game and 5.5 completed bounces. What a start!!! However, James wasn't someone who would let those hypes get into his head as he continued with a beautiful streak all through his stay at Cleveland. LeBron James following a fine start was the first Cleveland player to win the NBA rookie player of the year award and simultaneously the Third NBA player to have ever had an average of 20 points, 5 assists, and 5 rebounds per every game as a prep-to-pro player.

The period in-between 2004 – 2008 saw James quick rise to superstardom. He got his first NBA shirt in the All-Star selection in the year 2004/05. Everybody knew he wasn't just like every other basketball player, even critics went silent and various pundits had to acclaim to the fact that he was indeed a great player who would do exploits even at the young age of 20. He seemed to have an exceptional way of doing things differently from other Basketball players which was the very reason he was unique. The match against the Toronto Raptors on the 20th March, where LeBron scored a total of 56 points further justifies that he was indeed an exceptional players. That debut of his however, helped the Cleveland cleave a single record-breaking point but somehow wasn't enough for the team to make the playoff games in James's second consecutive season as Cleveland ended the season with a 42-40 record.

However, all these were not enough reasons to weigh down James zeal expertness for the basketball game as he helped East Conference achieve victory with an average 29 points in the 2006 All-Star game, thus winning the NBA Most Valuable Player (MVP) award in the competition. Known with his expertness toward leading, James led the Cavaliers to qualify for the playoffs for the first time since 1998. He also recorded a triple-double win against Washington Wizards before Detroit Pistons knock them out in the second round.

During the 2006/07 season, LeBron performances wasn't what it used to be. He had an average of 27.3 points, 6.7 rebounds, 6 assists, and 1.6 steals per game which was very different from his previous performances which was attributed to lack of focus and intensified effort, but James was human after-all.

One remarkable thing we cannot fail to point out is the remarks that came after the game as it was as eventful as it could be. During the Game 5 of the finals, James has successfully completed 48 points with 9 rebounds as well as having 7 assists. This wasn't all, he had scored virtually every point for his team, which included a winner debut against the Pistons. This game had gotten everyone present and watching to be on high attention.

The announcer at that time, Marv Albert has described the event as one of the greatest moments in post season basketball history. It didn't end there, every media wanted to identify with it. A commentator went out of his way to brand it in a Spanish way by referring to it as "Jordan-esque". News giant, *ESPN* wasn't left out of the drill, as though it took about six years to later tag it as the fourth greatest performance in Modern NBA history. However, Cleveland knew the hype surrounding them after such brilliant performance, so they stepped up their game and nailed the Game 6- to earn a place in the NBA finals against top-seeded, San Antonio Spurs. But it seemed they weren't meant for the championship title after all as they were knocked out with LeBron managing an average 22 points, 7.0 rebounds, and 6.8 assists with only 35.6% shooting,

During the 2007/08 season, James was upbeat once more amassing awards as he won the MVP for the All-Star Game for a second time with a 27-point, 8-rebound, and 9-assist enactment. On March 21, he moved past Brad Daugherty as the Cavaliers' all-time leading scorer in a game against the Raptors, doing so in over 100 less games than Daugherty. His 30 points for every game were likewise the most talked of in the team, which gave him his first scoring title. Notwithstanding his individual achievements, Cleveland's record tumbled from the prior year to 45– 37. Cleveland were rated as the fourth possible winners to win the East Conference playoffs and the Cavaliers crushed the Wizards in the first round for the third sequential season before being wiped out in seven games by the possible champion Boston Celtics in the following round. Amid the unequivocal seventh game in Boston, James scored 45 points and Paul Pierce scored 41 of every a game which the press depicted as a "shootout."

At the finish of the 2008– 09 season, James completed second in NBA Defensive Player of the Year voting and made his first NBA All-Defensive Team. He additionally turned out to be just the fourth post-merger player to led his team to securing more points through rebounds, steals, and blocks though the season. Behind his play and the securing of Elite player watch Mo Williams, Cleveland created another record 66– 16 and fell only one game shy of coordinating the best home record in history. With definite midpoints of 28.4 points, 7.6 bounce back, 1.7 steals, 7.2 assists and 1.2 blocks for every game, it was becoming more evident that James was the favorite to win the MVP Honor. Thinking about James' execution for ESPN, John Hollinger later expressed, "He's having what is ostensibly the best season ever, and it's obligatory we gave him his due for it.

In the playoffs, Cleveland defeated the Atlanta Hawks and Detroit Pistons to have a matchup with the Orlando Magic in the finals. In Game 1 of the series LeBron scored 49 points on 66 percent shooting in a losing exertion for the Cavaliers. In Game 2, he hit a shot to tie the series at 1– 1. Cleveland would lose the series in six games, and following the misfortune in Game 6, James quickly left the floor without shaking hands with others which was a demonstration that numerous media individuals saw as unsportsmanlike. For the arrangement, he had 38.5 points,

8.3 rebounds, and 8 assists, completing the post-season with a career playoff-high 35.3 points for each game.

In February of the 2009– 10 season, James was constrained into a transitory point monitor part following a progression of wounds to players in the Cavaliers' backcourt. With his excellent leadership, Cleveland had the best record in the league for the second season. Due to a limited extent to his expanded minutes as the Cavaliers' essential ball handler, James expanded his creation, averaging 29.7 points, 7.3 rebounds, 1.6 steals, 8.6 assists and 1 block for every game on 50 percent shooting on the way to another MVP Honor. Beginning the playoff on a better note, Cleveland beat the Bulls to secure a matchup with the Celtics in the second round. James was intensely censured for not playing great in Game 5, shooting just 20 percent on 14 shots and scoring 15 points. The team endured its most exceedingly awful misfortune in history and at the finish of the game, James strolled off the court to a sprinkling of boos from Cleveland's team. The Cavaliers were authoritatively dispensed with from the postseason in Game 6, with James posting 27 points, 10 assists, 19 rebounds, and nine turnovers in the losing exertion.

The Decision:

LeBron James has made his mark on the basketball court which is why every team wanted to sign him the moment he became a free agent. Different teams such as the Chicago Bulls, Los Angeles Lakers, Miami Heat, New Jersey Nets, and New York Knicks wanted to sign him to play for them. Even his old team, the Cavaliers, wanted to retain him. However, it was obvious that James had made up his mind to play for Miami Heats. Nonetheless, the move was much unexpected as it broke through every television series and various tongues were wagging but one thing everyone had in common in their mouth was alluding his move as a startling "DECISION" thus labelling as so on television station. But James knew what he was doing, he wanted to enjoy the game as much as he could and play less of the offensive style while making his impact on the court, and since the Miami Heat had made it clear that they would be signing fellow free agent Chris Bosh to add to Dwayne Wade's skills LeBron felt this would be the perfect fit for him. This move was rumored to be pre-planned as reports suggested that they had planned it way back in 2006. But in all actuality, James wanted to win the NBA championship and he felt he stood a better chance at winning with improved team mates where he didn't have to be the sole offensive star. However, the impact of Heat president Pat Riley couldn't be overlooked in trying to help James achieve his life-long dream as well as signing in for Miami Heats while playing with Bosh and Wade.

James leaving the Cavaliers drew controversy and was heavily criticized by virtually everyone from fans, former and present players, to sport pundits. The Decision seems to have been scrutinized and viewed as unnecessary. His action was seen not being professional enough that even former basketball world stars, Magic Johnson and Michael Jordan who labelled him as the guy who couldn't win the Championship without much help. Even his previous team owner, Dan Gilbert seemed not to have any of his antics and had to release his decries through an open letter while some fans made a public video of burning his Jersey. Following his transfer actions, he became one of America's most disliked Athletes.

James became an official Heats player on the 10th of July with a six year contract worth about, $110.1 million, a contract which saw him the third returning MVP to change teams and the first since Moses Malone in 1982. The Heats knew exactly the kind of player they signed and they knew they had to make him feel at home. In the evening of his arrival, he was given a welcome party along with the two other signings at the American Airlines Arena, where James proposed a toast to winning more championship titles.

What seem to be just a transfer turned out to be more serious than it seemed. The Heats were regarded as anti-heroes both through the media and fan bases, through the 2010-11 league season. To start the year, they attempted to change in accordance with these new conditions, going just 9– 8 after 17 games. James later conceded that the consistent cynicism encompassing the team influenced him to play with poor attitude. On December 2, James faced Cleveland where he scored 38 helped Miami secure a win while being booed each time he contacted the ball. The Heat ended the season well and completed as the East's second seed, with James averaging 26.7 points, 7.5 rebounds for each game with 51% shot.

In the playoffs, Miami Heats faced with the Celtics. In Game 5, he scored Miami's last ten points to help secure a win. After the game, he broadly stooped on the court in a passionate minute, later telling journalists that it was not just an individual triumph for him but for his team as well. The Heat inevitably progressed to the Finals, where they were subdued by Dallas Mavericks in Game 6. James got the brunt of the feedback for the loss averaging just three points in fourth quarters in the arrangement. His Finals scoring 17.8 points for every game implied a 8.9-point drop from the standard season, the biggest point drop-off in league history.

Consecutive championships (2011– 2013)

James was really affected by the Mavericks loss, and the experience propelled him to refocus on his play and love of the game, which helped him recapture a feeling of bliss on the court. He knew that his post-game required change, so he worked with Hakeem Olajuwon amid the offseason. During the 2011– 12 season, James had essentially extended his range of abilities which helped Miami start the year with an 18– 6 record. He was inevitably named MVP for the third time, while averaging 27.1 points on 53% shooting.

In January 2013, he became the youngest player in NBA history to score 20,000 points.

In the second round of the playoffs, Miami incidentally lost Chris Bosh to an upset stomach and wound up trailing the Indiana Pacers 2– 1. James had 40 points and 18 rebounds in Game 4 to help even the series. Miami defeated Pacers in Game 6 to win the series. In the next round against the Celtics, James scored 45 points to helping the Heat to triumph in what The New York Times called a "profession characterizing execution". Miami won Game 7 to progress to the Finals, acquiring them a matchup with the Oklahoma City Thunder and James' maturing rival, Kevin Durant. In the last stages of Game 4, James hit a three-pointer to give the Heat a lead, helping them win in spite of missing time with leg issues. He also enlisted a triple double as Miami vanquished Oklahoma City for their second championship. James was voted the NBA Finals Most Valuable Player with 28.6 points. His full postseason run, in which he averaged 30.3 points, is rated the second best in present day NBA history by ESPN.

In February of the 2012– 13 season, James averaged 29.7 points and 7.8 assists per game while setting numerous shooting effectiveness records. That same month, the Heat likewise started a 27-game winning streak, the third longest in NBA history. James' execution was depicted as a "month for the ages" by Sports Illustrated. Behind his play, Miami completed the year with an establishment and league best 66– 16 record, and James was named MVP for the fourth time, falling only one vote short of turning into the first player in NBA history to win the award unanimously.

In the playoffs James scored a buzzer beating layup to give Miami a one-point triumph against the Pacers. All through the arrangement, his supporting cast battled fundamentally, and his additional scoring load provoked him to contrast his obligations with those of his "Cleveland days". Regardless of these battles, the Heat progressed to the Finals for a rematch for James from his first Finals six years earlier. Toward the start of the arrangement, he was criticized for his absence of forcefulness and poor shot choice as Miami fell behind 2– 3. In Game 6, he recorded his second triple-double of the series, including 16 final quarter points, to lead the Heat to a rebound triumph. In Game 7, he tied the Finals record for most points scored in a Game 7 win, driving Miami over San Antonio with 37 points. He was named Finals MVP for the second year in a row, averaging 25.3 points, 10.9 rebounds, 7 assists, and 2.3 steals for every game in the championship series.

On the 3rd of March of the 2013– 14 season, James scored a professional record 61 points in a game against the Charlotte. While it was a tough year for the Heat due to injuries he still averaged 27.1 points, 6.4 assists and 6.9 rebounds. In the second round of the playoffs, he achieved postseason-high by scoring 49 points in Game 4 against the Brooklyn Nets. In the following round, Miami vanquished the Pacers to win their fourth back to back Finals appearance, getting to be one of just four teams in NBA history to do this. In Game 1 of the Finals, James missed most of the final quarter due to injuries giving the Spurs an early lead in the series. In Game 2, he drove the Heat to a tying triumph with 35 points on a 64 percent shooting rate. San Antonio in the end wiped out the Heat in five games, finishing Miami's mission for a three-peat. For the Finals, James found had 28.2 points, 7.8 rebounds, and 2.0 steals for every game.

Returning Home-HERE

On June 25, 2014, James wasn't willing to sign another contract with the Miami Heats and subsequently became a free. Unlike before, his declaration to come back to Cleveland was welcomed. On July 12, he formally signed with the team, who had incorporated a league-worst 97–215 record in the four seasons following his departure. Subsequently after his signing, the Cavaliers obtained Kevin Love from the Minnesota Timberwolves, alongside Kyrie Irving to complete an attacking trio.

But it seemed things weren't going to be as rosy as perceived for James as he was sidelined for two weeks due to injury in the 2014–15 season which was the most time sidelined in his career to date. But LeBron wasn't just a player, he was a superstar with vision as he came back from the injury to help Cleveland secure a 2-2 tie against the Bulls in the second round of the Playoffs. He was also significant in the victory over the Hawks in the Conference finals to progress to the final round against the Golden State Warriors. However, things took a drastic turn for Cleveland as two of their influential players, Irving and Love got relegated due to injury, leaving James with more offensive responsibilities. Although Cleveland later lost the series, they gave the Warriors a good run for their money to start in Game 1. James on his individual part was among the top performers to win the Finals MVP Award with an average of 35.8 points, 13.3 rebounds, and 8.8 assists throughout the championship game round.

Amid the 2015– 16 season, James was censured for his part in a few off-court discussions, including the midseason termination of Cavaliers' coach David Blatt. In spite of these issues, Cleveland completed the year with 57 wins and the best record in the East. James' averages were 25.3 points, 7.4 rebounds, and 6.8 assists per game on 52 percent shooting.

In the playoffs, the Cavaliers progressed easily to the Finals, losing just two games on the way to a rematch with the Warriors, who were coming off a record-setting 73 win season. To start the series Cleveland fell behind 3– 1. James reacted by enlisting consecutive 41 point games in Games 5 and 6, driving the Cavaliers to two sequential wins. In Game 7, he posted a triple double and made various key plays, including an essential run down on Andre Iguodala in the last two minutes, as Cleveland rose successful, winning the city's first pro athletics title in 52 years and became the first ever in NBA history to return from a 3– 1 shortfall in the Finals. James became the third player to record a triple-double out of a NBA Finals Game 7, and with 29.7 points, 11.3 rebounds, 8.9 assists, 2.3 squares, and 2.6 takes for per game. James also was the first league player in history to lead two teams in each of the five factual classes for a playoff round, coming full circle in a consistent Finals MVP.

The 2016– 17 season was defaced by wounds and startling misfortunes for the Cavaliers; James later depicted it as one of the "most interesting" years of his career. The Cavaliers completed the season as the East's second seed, with James averaging 26.4 points and record breaking rebounds (8.6), assists (8.7), and turnovers (4.1) per game. In Game 3 of the first round of the postseason, he enlisted 41 points, 13 rebounds, and 12 assists against the Pacers, driving Cleveland to rebound triumphal in the wake of trailing by 25 points at halftime, speaking to the biggest halftime comeback in NBA playoff history. In Game 5 of the Eastern Finals against the Celtics, James scored 35 points and outperformed Michael Jordan as the league's unequaled postseason scoring leader. The Cavaliers won and progressed to their third Finals against the Warriors. Behind averages of 33.6 points, 12 rebounds, and 10 assists for every game, James turned into the main player to normal a triple-double in the Finals, yet Cleveland was crushed in five games.

After the Cavaliers sold Kyrie Irving in the off-season transfer, Cleveland began the 2017– 18 season with a 3– 5 record. The following game, the Cavaliers crushed the Washington Wizards 130– 122. James scored 57 points in the game to set the second-highest point totals of his career. James came to no less than 10 points for the 800th game in succession, joining Michael Jordan (866) as the other NBA player with a streak that long. James additionally turned into the youngest player to reach 29,000 NBA career points.

On December 16, 2017, he had his 60th career triple-double in a 109– 100 win against the Utah Jazz. James had his fifth triple-double of the season and passed Larry Bird for 6th position in his career. On January 23, 2018, following a 114– 102 to the San Antonio, James turned into the seventh player in NBA history to record 30,000 points. At 33, James was the youngest player to score 30,000— Kobe Bryant was 34 years and 104 days he recorded such feat.

On February 27, 2018, James scored 31 points and completed an average triple-double, beating Brooklyn Nets 129– 123. James also had 12 rebounds and 11 assists for his twelfth triple-double of the season and 67th of his career. He achieved 8,000 assists amid the game to become the first NBA player in history to achieve 30,000 points, 8,000 rebounds and 8,000 assists. On March 30, 2018, in a 107–102 win against the Pelicans, James scored in his 867th straight game, breaking Michael Jordan's long-standing record. During the 2018 NBA Playoffs, James was named to the All-NBA First Team for the twelfth straight year, denoting another NBA record. With the Cavaliers crushing the Boston Celtics 87– 79 in Game 7 of the Eastern Confrence Finals, James achieved the NBA Finals for the eighth straight year, which no player had done since individuals from the early Celtics dynasty did in the 60s. In Game 1 of the NBA Finals, James scored 51 points to go along with eight assists and eight rebounds in a 124– 114 overtime loss. James turned out to be just the 6th player to ever score no less than 50 points in a NBA Finals game. This additionally was his eighth game of no less than 40 points in the 2018 playoffs and tied Jerry West's accomplishment in 1965 for most in a postseason series. On June 29, 2018, James officially refused to sign another contract with Cavaliers and opened himself up to free agency.

New playing challenges.

On July 9, James signed a $154 million contract with the Los Angeles Lakers. Just within three months, his jersey sales experienced an over 600 percent spike contrasted with his Cavaliers jersey upon his arrival to Cleveland in July 2014.

Rebuilding A Program: LeBron's Contributions to Team USA

James made his first international debut for the US national team at the 2004 Olympics in Athens, Greece. He was however not given a large amount of playing time, averaging 14.6 minutes with 5.8 points and 2.6 rebounds in every game. The team finished third in the competition clinching the bronze and became the first US team to return home without the gold medal after adding dynamic NBA players to their line-up. James felt his restricted playing time was a "lowlight" and frustrated he was not given the chance to play. His outburst in the Olympics competition was depicted as "insolent" and "disagreeable" by reporters Adrian Wojnarowski and Dwindle Vecsey.

At the 2006 FIBA game in Japan, James was the co-captain in the USA team and but still had 13.9 points, 4.8 rebounds, and 4.1 assists throughout the game. The team completed the competition with an 8– 1 record, winning another bronze award. James' conduct was again scrutinized, this time by Bruce Bowen, who defied James amid tryouts about his involvement with the team staff.

Before naming James to the 2008 Olympic team, The USA team overseeing executive Jerry Colangelo and Coach Mike Krzyzewski gave James a final offer to enhance gameplay and he paid attention to their recommendation. At the FIBA Americas Championship 2007, he was able to amass a total of 18.1 points, 3.6 rebounds, and 4.7 assists for every game, including a 31-point game against Argentina in the championship, breaking the record as the first American to achieve such a feat in an Olympic qualifier. The national team went ahead to win gold in the competition with a 10– 0, streak in preparation for the 2008 Olympics in Beijing, China. James credited the team's mentality and experience for their change, paying respect to the national team's color. In the last game, James turned in 14 points 6 bounce back, with an additional of 3 assists against Spain

James did not feature at the 2010 FIBA game but played with the national team in the 2012 Olympics in London. He was the leader of the team alongside with Kobe Bryant. James helped the offense from the post and border, called the cautious sets, and scored when he deemed fit. In a game against Australia, he had a record of triple-double in U.S. Olympic basketball history with 11 points, 14 rebounds and more than 10 assists. The national team won gold again crushing Spain in the last game. In the final game against Spain, James had 19 points thus becoming America's all-time leading scorer in men's Olympic basketball history. He ended up tallying with Michael Jordan as the ones to win a NBA MVP award, NBA championship, NBA Finals MVP, and gold in the Olympics game. Not too long after, former critics like Krzyzewski were forced to shower him praises, naming the best basketball player in history.

Numerous basketball pundits mentors, fans, and even players see James as one of the best players ever. Since 2011, he has been ranked the best player in the NBA by ESPN and other sports related magazine and TV series. He has continually won the All-NBA award every season since his second year, defensive awards each season from 2009 to 2014, and was named Youngster of the Year in his first season. With four MVP awards, he has won the award four times which is on par with the likes of Kareem Abdul-Jabbar, Jordan, and Bill Russell; James and Russell are the two players who have won four MVP awards in a five-year span. James has never won the Defensive Player of the Year Award, however he has twice completed second in the voting and records the award as one of his fundamental objectives. James has showed up in the Finals nine times and won three championships. A few examiners have scrutinized him for not having a superior Finals record, while others have guarded him, contending that even if James performed well, his team was crushed by a dominant team.

Playing Offensively

Being a deft finisher, James has led the NBA in scoring and shooting percentages at the edge in 2013.

James entered the NBA as an 18-year-old new kid on the block and had a prompt offensive effect when he drove the Cavaliers in scoring. He holds various "youngest to" qualifications, including being the youngest player to score 28,000 professional points. Amid his first spell in Cleveland, he was essentially utilized as an on-ball point forward. His shooting inclinations are well bordered, and he set up himself as outstanding amongst other finishers in ball; he was the NBA's leading player in the three-point shots in 2006.

His blend of speed, agility, and size frequently made matchup issues for contradicting teams since he was fit for passing up bigger guards and overwhelming smaller players. These characteristics turned out to be more obvious experiencing significant change, where he built up notoriety for getting defensive rebounds and after that beating the defense down court for highlight-quality baskets. Around this time, James was reprimanded for not having a dependable jump shot or post-game. Teams would attempt to abuse these shortcomings by giving him space in the half court and forcing him to make due with three-pointers and long two-pointers, a methodology broadly used by Spurs in the 2007 Finals.

James' playmaking capacity is by and large thought to be one of his chief aptitudes, with a few experts positioning him among the best passers in NBA history. He is the main frontcourt player in league history and is responsible for more than 7,000 professional assists. Being blessed with size vision, and the attention he collects from defenses further bolsters his passing, James can make simple points for his teammates with precise assists, producing a league leading 2.6 three-pointers per game by passing alone in 2013. He has frequently executed passes that would regularly be viewed as unusual, including passes after leaving his feet and going through defense. His uncanny inclination to locate a free player has being very noteworthy in his advancement of NBA defenses, which powers teams to consolidate a few area components into their plans to better cover the frail side of the court and keep James from going to open shooters.

LIFE OFF THE COURT

James married his high school love, Savannah Brinson, on September 14, 2013 in San Diego, California. Together, they are blessed with three children, LeBron James Jr., Bryce Maximus James, and Zhuri James. Amid his spell with the Heat, James dwelled in Coconut Grove, where he purchased a $9 million three-story chateau sitting above Biscayne Bay. In November 2015, James purchased a 9,350 square-foot East Coast– style chateau in Brentwood, Los Angeles for about $21 million.

James is considered by numerous individuals, including his kindred NBA players, to be the "substance of the NBA". His sentiments have yielded noteworthy impact on individuals who settle on vital league decisions; for instance, in 2014 he requested that Chief Adam Silver increase the length of the All-Star break, and the demand was put into place the next season. On February 13, 2015, James was chosen the principal VP of the National Basketball Players Affiliation (NBPA).

Media figure and business interests

James is represented by agent, Rich Paul of Klutch Sports. Aaron Goodwin, who was his first ever agent whom he cleared out in 2005 for Leon Rose. Rose joined Creative Artists Agency (CAA) in 2007, and he worked with CAA operator Henry Thomas, who spoke with Dwyane Wade and Chris Bosh, to sign James to Miami Heats. James left CAA for Paul in 2012. James, Paul, Maverick Carter, and Randy Mims—all cherished companions—shaped operator and sports-showcasing organization LRMR after James left

Goodwin. LRMR handles James' promoting, including the showcasing of The Decision, for which it was criticized.

All through his career, James has been positioned by Forbes as one of the world's world best athletes, and in 2017, the US Time magazine recorded him as one of the 100 most powerful individuals alive. Amid his first spell with the Cavaliers, he was venerated by neighborhood fans, and Sherwin-Williams displayed a mammoth Nike-created standard of James on its home office. In spite of their love for James, Cleveland fans and pundits were as often irritated when he wore a Yankees cap when he went to Cleveland Indians ball games versus the New York Yankees. Following his activities amid the 2010 free agent period and, all the more particularly, The Decision, he was recorded as one of the world's most hated competitors. By 2013, his picture had mostly recuperated and he was accounted for by ESPN as the most well-known player in the NBA for the second time in his vocation.

All through his profession, James has adopted a remarkable strategy to his NBA contracts, for the most part picking to sign shorter-term bargains to expand his profit potential and adaptability; for instance, in 2006, he and the Cavaliers entered a three-year deal worth $60 million contract expansion rather than the four-year as it gave him the choice of looking for a different contract worth more cash as an unlimited free role following the 2010 season. This move at last permitted James, Dwyane Wade, and Chris Bosh to sign with the Heat together. Amid his second stretch in Cleveland, he started quitting and re-marking on new contracts after each season so as to exploit higher compensations coming about because of the NBA's rising salary cap. In 2016, he signed with the Cavaliers on a three-year bargain, turning into the highest-paid player in the league.

James has signed various advertising deals; a portion of the organizations that he has worked with are Coca-Cola, Dunkin' Brands, McDonald's, Nike, and Beats by Dre. Leaving high school, he was the prize of a three-way offering war among Nike, Reebok, and Adidas, in the end marking with Nike for around $90 million. His shoes have helped Nike continue their dominance in the basketball shoe market. In 2011, Fenway Sports Team turned into the bottom worldwide advertiser of his rights, and as a major aspect of the plan he was conceded a minority stake in the English Head League football club Liverpool, who he has asserted his help for. Because of James' support cash and NBA compensation, he has been recorded as one of the world's highest-paid competitors. In 2013, he outperformed Kobe Bryant as the highest paid basketball player on the planet, with profit of $56.5 million. In 2014, James made more profits worth more than $30 million as a feature of Apple's procurement of Beats Hardware; he had initially struck an arrangement to get a little stake in the organization at its beginning in return for advancing its earphones. In 2015, he was rated the 6th highest earning sportsperson, and third highest in 2016 - after football superstars, Lionel Messi and Cristiano Ronaldo. James has expressed that he might want to claim a NBA team later on.

James and comic Jimmy Kimmel co-hosted the 2007 ESPY Awards. In other comedic interests, he hosted the 33rd-season debut of Saturday Night Live. He has likewise attempted his hand at acting, showing up in an appearance on the HBO show Escort. In 2015, he played himself in the Judd Apatow film Trainwreck, getting positive reviews for his performance. That same year, James' advanced video organization which generated $15.8 million from Warner Bros.

James and his business accomplice Maverick Carter co-own a production organization whose first work was the Lions Gate production "More than a Game" released in 2009 and chronicled James' high school years. Some other series released by SpringHill incorporate the Disney XD sports documentaries, Becoming, Starz sitcom Survivor's Regret, and an animated video, The LeBrons. In 2016, CNBC publicized an unscripted series facilitated by James called Cleveland Hustles, where four best in class Northern Ohio business people will be financed on the state of rejuvenating an area in Cleveland. In the 2017 Toronto International Film festival had an hour long Vince Carter narrative entitled The Carter effect was official delivered by James and Maverick Carter alongside rappers Drake and Future. In February 2018 it was reported that James' organization will produce another film in the Party series with James anticipated to appear.

Activism

James is an active supporter of non-profit associations, including After-School All-Stars, Boys and Girls Clubs of America, Defense club for children, and ONEXONE. He likewise has his own philanthropy foundation, the LeBron James Family Foundation, which is situated in Akron. Since 2005, the foundation has held a yearly a-thon to fund-raise for different causes. In 2015, James had an organization with the College of Akron to give grants to

CPSIA information can be obtained
at www.ICGtesting.com
Printed in the USA
LVHW040917011218
598888LV00003B/774/P